W9-BQL-883

Dick and Jane

READING COLLECTION • VOLUME 7

Away We Go

GROSSET & DUNLAP • NEW YORK

Tim

Jump up, Sally.

Jump up.

Come, Sally.

Jump up.

Jump up, Tim.

Jump up.

Up, up, up.

Jump up.

Look, Dick.

See Sally and Tim.

Funny, funny Sally.

Funny, funny Tim.

Tim and Spot

Go, Tim.

Go up.

Go up, Tim.

Go up, up, up.

Go, Tim.

Go down.

Go, go, go.

Go down.

Go down, down, down.

Oh, Jane.

See Spot and Tim.

See Spot run.

See funny Spot.

See funny Tim.

Up, Tim

Up Puff, up.
Come Puff, come.

Oh, oh.

See Puff jump down.

Up Puff, up.

Jump up, Puff.

Jump up.

14

See Tim.

Up, Tim, up.

Run Away Spot

"Oh, Spot," said Jane.
"You can not play here."

Jane said, "I can make a house."

"I can make a little house,"
said Jane.

Dick said, "I can make a house.
A big house for two boats.
A house for the yellow boat.
And for the blue boat.
See my big house."

Jane said, "I can make a house.
A big house for three cars.
Red and blue and yellow cars."

Sally said, "I can make a house.

A little house for Tim.

Here is my house for Tim.

Tim is in it.

Tim can play in it.

Oh, oh, oh.

Tim looks funny in the house."

"See my house," said Dick.
"Down it comes."

"See my house," said Jane.
"Down, down it comes."

"Oh, oh, oh," said Sally.
"Down comes my little house.
Run away, Puff.
Run away, Spot.
You can not play here."

Away We Go

Sally said, "Away we go.
Away we go in the car.
Mother and Father.
Dick and Jane.
Sally and Tim."

Dick said, "Spot is not here.
Puff is not here."

Dick said, "I see something.
Look down, Jane.
Look down and see something.
It is funny.
Can you see it?"

"Oh, oh," said Jane.
"Here is Spot."

"Come in, Spot," said Jane.
"You can go in the car."

"Away we go," said Sally.
"Away we go in the car.
Mother and Father.
Dick and Jane.
Sally and Tim and Spot.
Away we go in the big, big car."

See It Go

Jane said, "Look, look.
I see a big yellow car.
See the yellow car go."

Sally said, "I see it.
I see the big yellow car.
I want to go away in it.
I want to go away, away."

Dick said, "Look up, Sally.
You can see something.
It is red and yellow.
It can go up, up, up.
It can go away."

Sally said, "I want to go up.
I want to go up in it.
I want to go up, up, up.
I want to go up and away."